DE MAYOR OF HARLEM

De Mayor of Harlem

The Poetry of

David Henderson

E. P. Dutton & Co., Inc.   New York   1970

First Edition

Published simultaneously in Canada by
Clarke, Irwin & Company Limited, Toronto and Vancouver

Library of Congress Catalog Card Number: 77-95471

SBN 0-525-03248-7 (Paper)   SBN 0-525-08996-9 (Cloth)

Grateful acknowledgment is hereby made to the following publications in which some of these poems have appeared: *Umbra, New American Review, In Transit, Boss Magazine, American, National Guardian, Kaleidoscope, Freedomways, Los Angeles Free Press, Negro Digest, Evergreen Review, Fiba: Actualité,* and *First Issue.*

To Barbara, Henry,
and Ma and Pa

Contents

De Mayor of Harlem

1962–1966

Walk with De Mayor of Harlem

I

enter harlem
to walk from the howling cave
called the "A" train /
from columbus circle
                (find america discovered)
all along a 66 block artillery blitz
                          to the quarter /
      nonstop
      existential TWA nightcoach
rome to auschwitz express
where multitudes vomit   pass out
witness death by many stabbings
upon pompeii /
        please close the doors please
before the madness of washington heights
     disembark   / silent moot   of black vectors
to sunder this quarter
          thru

black mass
black land

-of rhythm n
         blues & fish of jesus frying across the boardwalk
snake dancers walk mojo along wide boulevards
sight for those
        who live away
a new land!
no dream stuff
   in dem black neon clouds of de full moon
         to illume by sun-ra
streets just like you
        no thinking you crazy

vertigo
         under skyscrapers /

         II

where harlem lies
              find no industrial green
                              giants
only
       bojangling children in the streets
only
       the sleeping car brotherhood of underground males
only
       the knights of the mystic sea
find only
              the black sapphires
              of the beulah baptist methodist church on the
                                          mount
here
       clustered & cross-purposed

                        you can take it where you find it
                        or you can leave it like it is

walk with de mayor of harlem
find no   find no
                  find not
many of the millions
   of the downtown boston blackies
fancy of james bond
in psychedelic robert hall clothing
suitable drape for sawed-off
shotguns
under the trench coat

talk to me   talk to me
                   tell me like it is
the memory   of sky watch
sun dance   drum chant   body-ruba

taut are the signals thru the skin
thru bones
hard as the forgotten legions
of
the giant bushmen

O beulah baptist in the streets /
to the paradise songs of bloodletting
the gospel singers   are   asayin /
the world is in a troubled time
when
        the knights of the mystic sea
clash
        with the sicilian asphalt paving company
a blood ruckus
                will ensue
that night
there will be monsoon rains over harlem
black panther bonnevilles prowling
from block to block
helicopters colliding with tenements
                        in orange surprise

Bopping

My main men and I bopped
to general agreement (like the toast to "the boys upstate"
                         before every bottle of Paradise or
                         Thunderbird wine)
down cats
we bopped to give cause to the causes
that died before they got to us.

I remember the arm-pumping cap-crowned blades
of my boyhood
their elemental gait talking
deep beneath my eyes . . .
the list at waist and trunk ˙
          whip of an arm
& abrupt   then long wing-tipped stride
of days when we had to show ourselves love
in difficult pretensions
          as if speaking words of self-love
          was too remote   a performance
     when   before the fact
we understood all too well
the action of the thrust.

We maneuvered
to turn that way in dawns or dusk
of the eternal wars
among ourselves   our gangs:
          the Seven Crowns   Chaplins   Sportsmen   Egyptian Knights
Boston Baldies   Young Sinners   Enchanters   Duschon Lords—
because talking   after all   is too little of glamour
to the hungry   the ugly   the mean

We bopped when about to fight
and we bopped when happy
all in our own slight variances
known to the members of the Road

and known to the similar bops
of the roaming hordes

From Avenue "D" to Red Hook
thru Marcy Projects   then Crown Heights
Prospect Avenue in the Bronx & also in Brooklyn
The Fifth Avenue Armory on 141st & the Harlem River
Bronx River Housing   forty-three   fifty-five
99 center Boston Road
From winters to graduation
From street duels
until
wedlock   or the cops
shot us down
bopping . . .

So We Went to Harlem

To Richard Valentine
and Cal Hernton

I

So we went to Harlem.
The many-fabled lettermen—two blacks, one white—
Went to Harlem to get some pussy.

Roaring through the streets
—me driving—
Hood flying off on Park Avenue
—me choking with laughter.
Cal blasting Spanish at Puerto Ricans
Coming from dance.   One sauntering over,
Cal mitigating, *Que pasa?* man.
Que pasa?   sweetly flowing.

Three thorns
Precipitous
For the drain
Coming from a Brooklyn Beatnik party
Drunk
                    happy
            and full of sap

                —going to Harlem!

David at the wheel high driving like a speed-gone fool
Flawing greatly guffawing . . . gently leaking
Richard laughing in spasms   Cal cajoling before arriving
And me passing the wine in that rollicking Plymouth
So light
So gay
On the verge of flight but not over
That ghetto
            Goin' to see your baby?
            Naw! goin to HARLEM—*get some broads!*

18

II

So we cantered into Harlem rambling the car apark
On some glittering street . . .
HARLEM!   Where I was spawned
            Where Richard was labeled
            Where Calvin is to gasp to his death.

So we arrived in Harlem!
Up and down 125th Street
            126th Street
            127th Street
            128th, 129th   . . . *up and down*
—*Looking for a good time, boys?*
                        up and down
—*Eight dollahs all you need. Any broad you want!*
                        up and down
—*What's happenin' fellas?*
                        up and down
—*Hey!*
                        up and down
        (I ask white Richard if he likes any
        special one. He doesn't know.)
                        up and down
—*What's your name sweetheart.*
                        up and down
        BABY! HONEY! SWEETHEART! LOVER!
up
        BROADS—ASSES—BUTTER—BROWN—HEAVEN! . . .
        the sweeter the berry—

                                    down
Across and below   *. . . across and below*

Woman (a black hostess) approaches eyes on Richard
She ask if he would like to come with her.   Richard
*un*articulate looks to me—Gunga Din
Cal's off somewhere
Richard doesn't speak

19

Silence implies negation
business law?
(but of course may imply
affirmation—depending on
the circumstance)
Could silence under obligation to speak imply guilt?
Woman leaves at my power of attorney
Richard ruminates
Cal returns
Richard decides he wants her
I obtain   —David the Pimping Rinehart—no
Commission . . . Please!

Richard meets broad formally, is enchanted and strolls
Away with Atavistic visions of ghetto copulation.
Calvin and I joy for strange dissimilar reasons.

Long time later when Richard should have reached that
Fulsome orgasm we find him still walking the streets,
Have not yet commemorated but still happy-faced.
The Woman:
Round semblance of the fine shit-talking and Oblique to
the sap that coagulates at the Portress never to flow—
Richard
White strange goofy deep-in-love: giggling cuddle kiss
Smile   high   —too deep . . . will never
lose love to a ghetto

III

So in going to Harlem and being meandered throughout
We: the chick, Richard, Cal and I
Getting Black
Market wine.   Cal talking nigger-shit, Richard jealous
Of his tax-free purchase.   Cal cajoling at last
To the final reluctance.   Me sopping wine and dripping,
Knowing Richard's fate   Not knowing if I felt exultation
Pain or guilt   submitting generously to the wine—

IV

So we left Harlem
After Richard had been taken at last to some hotel
And told by the broad to wait outside while she
"arranged things" and Richard waiting and trusting
      And waiting . . .

Cal and I finally found Richard wandering about
The same block lost and looking.   Richard having
Given the hustler all of his money and ours, to
The ghetto he trusted and winding up lost.
Richard being lost for one hour and saying in the car
On the way back to the Village that he still liked her.
Richard
Lost once in a ghetto
So he who went to Harlem will never lose love to a ghetto
Richard
Who loved one night a ghetto
Richard
Who sat in the speeding car very much confused
And didn't help retrieve the hood when it flew off again
Cal thinking
And David
Driving too hard to think . . .

"Pope Arrives in New York City
Broadway Hustlers Go Wild"

For John Harriman

Here comes
The Pope off the Queensborough bridge
& uptown /   to harlem
  just like Castro did in '60
  Castro ate barbecued chicken
  prepared on the floor
  The Pope is a light eating gourmet
  coffee every meal
  troubled sleep   / caffeine dreams

a spry sixty-eight yr old man
what exercises must he perform   / by nervous sun-up?

gentle man   compassion his eyes
seeing everywhere
    having been before
    to the troubled apparitions
    of western whites grabbing his robe
     kissing his ring
     gimme that blessing   / they stay
       wretched
     ignorant of magicians

gentle man mendicant his robes
 white gleam arms-up body arch
gliding swords turn
to wands
   red & white aura
   of pale passionate man
   clutched by Cardinal Spellman
   an uninspired jimminy cricket

the Pope is like James Baldwin
only the latter's magic

22

is closer to the skin
J.B. says "hey baby"
& embraces with others often

The Pope is a weird motorcade
more weird than Marcello's journey to the Madonna
or Fellini's carnival
                    NOW HERE IS THE POPE!
"Blessings Italian Style"
                              (produced by Joseph E. Levine)

the Pope is preceded and followed
by late model USA convertibles
straight from Hertz
creamy blue   ocean green
official occasion black
preceding Pope a motorcycle wedge
of New York City's "Hells Angels" police force
the protected Pope follows
a diminished silver red bubble top
surrounds his skull

black cars   grinning city officials anonymous
gawking eyes straining over crowd
secret service men   / former college football stars
piled over detergent colored convertibles
crude in the streets
                    "AMERICA UNABLE TO TAKE POPE
                       INELEGANCE EVERYWHERE"
the police follow
in their souped up secondhand taxicabs
& emergency trucks
                    strobic beams turned off—
over TV president andrew lyndon johnson
in his rocking chair
leans towards the Pope
gesturing like Kingfish

("THE VATICAN PAVILION SECOND ONLY TO

GENERAL MOTORS IN WORLD FAIR ATTENDANCE
THE PIETA WILL NEVER LEAVE ROME AGAIN!")

here pope   there pope
walking around
seeing the sites
bowing   gesturing
greatly
        does not he know
      how old men are treated
    in america

Anniversary (George Washington's Birthday / 1967)

brothers & sisters
today
    you will hear
the exploding guns
the collapsing chairs
the fallen man   —El Malik / arise!
today
fusillades across the universe

Sprinkle Goofer Dust

& the courts will cut yr dick
facing the tester
no pussy in the penal code

the vigilantes of the black light
will have you ten to twenty
enclaved in yr storing semen

& come out semen snap-strength
along the genetic tune of the backbone
cobra sway to harlem jass
jump like malcolm

Saga of the Audubon Murder

brothers and sisters
we are gathered here today
to recommemorate
the assassination of malcolm x
our assassin historians
have placed us here
among the remnants
of george washington's
birthday party
> *but somehow*
> *we cannot recall*
> *the revolution*

somehow
all we can remember of american history
is the clatter of gunfire
in the audubon ballroom
the chest-bared screams
of malcolm of all of us
over backwards in blood
> *so much blood in this soil*
> *we all gonna turn red*
> > *someday*

Psychedelic Fireman

Psychedelic fireman
all over america
      New York City / Babylon
everyone high
meat of animals
tropical sugars
LSD   crime
america is a land of drug addicts
ones who have blown their minds
historically locking up the mellow

/ crime in the streets
a slogan

walk his city by sundown
witness
flames upon rooftops
along the piers
palisades crumbling spires
organized amusement parks   / fright-death
upon roller coasters with one end   only
passengers fall out backwards
into mad carnival music of the streets
sirens imported from druid regions of europa
worldwide police believe them
the weirdest
roller coaster through manhattan by underground express
iron cars trains of auschwitz
jangling metal grit   subway air

MAN DOES NOT BELONG UNDERGROUND
yet the blue men
of the eerie druid regions
      patrol in place of dogs mad
metal   iron symphony   insanity
      to dope-heads no matter

strobe-beam police cars swirling at subway entrance
"oh my god, not another subway crime!"
underground housewives scream in despair
women waiting to be raped by the "A" train
fast metal shaft
black native express
sweatdripping cars   drooping ubangi lips   / waiting for the haul
from midtown 59th
to harlem 125th
sixty-six blocks
of pillage /   shrieking white women of washington heights
mass rape of ornette
the trumpet boy

GENERAL MOTORS WORLD FAIR ATTENDANCE
TOPS VATICAN PAVILION

AMERICA!
   is a land of speeding cars
          drapes the moon
phosphorus   fart fire burns   carbohydrates
racist sugar   napalm-whiskey

speeding cars
lights white green flicker
               white lightning
                  along highways & underground tubes
huge poster signs
          wood posters billboard platters neon
                  phallic & decaying
red devil paint   / alcoholic   white light
upon fluorescence
               versus sky
               king   blue

PLASTER WALLS DON'T BURN
               they say
firemen flashing from posters

reeling from billboards
clutching little girls
moby dick his eyes
mommy her mouth
        fireman leers
I HAVE SAVED THIS LITTLE GIRL IN NAME OF THE STATE
KEEP NEW YORK PLASTERED

face of fire
methedrine skin erosion pop
flashing white crystals
        lining streets   / white Xmas
blaze   out strobe beam   swing   black   light
camera weird focus
       intrepid fireman
           hands up little girl's dress
fireman reels
intrepid child does not scream
collapsing walls
sirens high dog howl /   end of a mother's scream prolonged
           in the hearts of our countrymen
       door burst   flailing axes
swords   saxophones
broken back furniture   smoke   fire   wood

        WHILE
    thru Harlem fire rages water cycles
       weekends of fun / partying / burning flesh
       this thanksgiving
   for the natives   who hunt for the feast
   but do not partake /
           silent natives screaming
           thru western guns swords axes
             tall tenor saxophones
   blaring black trumpets / pages of swords
           spanish habana
           African chants / long-legged dance
    to the bullfight

29

                    stab the beast
              don't waste a stroke by spear
              symbolic death for your meat /
          harlem raging
                  trumpet tenor axes blare
          MIDNIGHT HOUR
                      / sugar shards high music
                  to tumult of psychedelic
          artillery
                              of cities insane /

Keep on Pushing

(Harlem Rebellion, Summer 1964—A Documentary)

The title and excerpts are taken from a hit recording
(summer, 1964) by the famous rhythm and blues trio—
Curtis Mayfield and the Impressions.

I

Lenox Avenue is a big street
The sidewalks are extra wide—three and four times
    the size of a regular Fifth Avenue or East 34th
    sidewalk—and must be so to contain the
    unemployed
vigiling Negro males,
and police barricades.

The Police Commissioner can
muster five hundred cops in five minutes
He can summon extra
tear-gas bombs / guns / ammunition
within a single call
to a certain general alarm /
For Harlem
reinforcements come from the Bronx
just over the three-borough bridge /
    a shot   a cry   a rumor
can muster five hundred Negroes
from idle and strategic street corners
    bars   stoops   hallways   windows
Keep on pushing.

II

I walk Harlem
I see police eight to a corner
crude mathematics
eight to one

eight for one
I see the white storeowners and the white keepers
and I see the white police force
The white police in the white helmets
and the white proprietors in their white shirts
talk together and
look around.

I see black handymen put to work because of the riots
boarding up smashed storefronts
They use sparkling new nails
The boards are mostly fresh hewn pine
and smell rank fresh.
The pine boards are the nearest Lenox Avenue will
    ever have to trees.
    Phalanxes of police
march   up and down
They are   dispatched   and   gathered   helmet heads
Bobbing white black and blue
They walk around   squadroned and platooned
groups of   six   eight   twelve.
Even in a group
the sparse black cop walks alone
or with a singular
talkative
white buddy.
          Keep on pushing

     III

I walk and the children playing frail street games seem
like no other children anywhere
they seem unpopular   foreign
as if in the midst of New York civilization existed
a crytic and closed society.
    Am I in Korea?
I keep expecting to see
companies of camouflage-khakied marines
the Eighth Army

Red Crosses—a giant convoy
Down the narrow peopled streets
jeeps with granite-face military men
marching grim champions of the Free World
Trucks dispensing Hershey bars   Pall Malls
medical equipment
nurses doctors drugs serums to treat
the diseased and the maimed
and from the Harlem River
blasting whistles horns
volleying firebombs against the clouds
the 7th Fleet . . .

      but the prowling Plymouths
      and helmeted outlaws from Queens
      persist.
            Keep On A'Pushing

      IV

I see the plump pale butchers pose with their signs:
    "Hog maws 4 pounds for 1 dollar"
    "Pigs ears 7 pounds for 1 dollar"
    "Neckbones   chitterlings   6 pounds for 1"
    Nightclubs,   liquor stores   bars 3, 4, 5 to one block
3 & 4 shots for one dollar
I see police eight to one
    in its entirety Harlem's 2nd law of Thermodynamics
        Helmet
        nightsticks bullets to barehead
        black reinforced shoes to sneaker
Am I in Korea?

      V

At night Harlem sings and dances
And as the newspapers say:
they also pour their whiskey on one another's heads.

They dog and slop in the bars
The children monkey in front of Zero's Records Chamber
on 116th and Lenox
They mash potatoes and madison at the Dawn Casino,
Renaissance Ballroom, Rockland Palace, and the Fifth
    Avenue Armory
on 141st and the Harlem River.

—*Come out of your windows*

dancehalls, bars and grills   Monkey   Dog   in the street
like Martha and the Vandellas
Dog for NBC
The Daily News and *The New York Times*
Dog for Andrew Lyndon Johnson
and shimmy a bit
for "the boys upstate"
and the ones in Mississippi
                    Cause you got soul
                    Everybody knows . . .
                    Keep on Pushin'

            VI

This twilight
I sit in Baron's Fish & Chip Shack
Alfonso (the counterman) talks of ammunition
The *Journal-American* in my lap
headlines promise EXCLUSIVE BATTLE PHOTOS
by a daring young photographer they call Mel Finkelstein
through him they insure "The Face of Violence—The
    Most Striking Close-ups" /
WWRL the radio station that serves
the Negro community
tools along on its rhythm n blues vehicle
The colorful unison announcers
declare themselves "The most soulful station in the nation"

Then the lecture series on Democracy comes on
The broadcaster for this series doesn't sound soulful
(eight to one he's white, representing management)
We Negroes are usually warned of the evils of Communism
and the fruits of Democracy / but this evening he tells us
that / in this troubled time we must keep our heads
and our Law
and our order (and he emphasizes order)
he says violence only hurts (and he emphasizes hurts)
     the cause of freedom and dignity /   He urges the troubled
restless residents of Harlem and Bedford-Stuyvesant to stay in
their homes, mark an end to the tragic and senseless violence
a pause
then he concludes
"Remember
     this is the land of the free"
and a rousing mixed chorus ends with the majestic harmony of
     "AND THE HOME OF THE BRAVE . . ."

Alfonso didn't acknowledge
he hears it every hour on the hour.
The Rhythm n Blues returns
a flaming bottle bursts on Seventh Avenue
and shimmies the fire across the white divider line
helmets
and faces white as the fluorescence of the streets
bob by
Prowl cars speeding wilding wheeling
the loony turns of the modulating demodulating sirens
climb the tenements window by window
Harlem moves in an automatic platform
The red fish lights swirl the gleaming storefronts
there will be no Passover this night
and then again the gunfire high
in the air   death static
          over everything . . .
ripped glass
shards   sirens   gunfire

down towards 116th
    as Jocko scenes radio WWRL

late at night Jocko hustles wine: Italian Swiss Colony Port
sherry and muscatel.   Gypsy Rose and Hombre "The
    Man's Adult Western Wine"
but by day and evening
his raiment for Harlem's head is different
zealous Jocko coos forward
his baroque tongue
snakes like fire
                    "Headache?
                        . . . take Aspirin
                    Tension?
                        . . . take Compōz!"

    Keep on pushin'
    Someway somehow
    I know we can make it
    With just a little bit of soul.

—————

sirens
     in   the lower east side
                             night
muster
     of winter fires
will surely wake
the children

—————

Black rascal
          blue max
is an elevator operator
holding
either
     a forty-five
     or a reefer

Yarmuul Speaks of the Riots

the time has come
I am taking my paintings to europe—Here
the opposition will destroy them
—i read from my diary
of the coming conflict
why it must be /
you see its a *feeling*
its not logic
a feeling
its not thought out
you say nows the time
black people got nothing to lose
i sit here
i am thinking of what i got to do
i send my family back to europe
i am not even born here
i am a black dutchman
but   i am also a man of color
        the third world
        has got to stand now
i got to be here
to see   this thing   go down
do what i can /

Marcus Garvey Parade

from their gray stone
   unfinished building
   the marcus garveyites
             stand in formation
             black army
BLACK & GOLD UNIFORMED BLACKS BLASTING
   DRUMS SOUND
BLASTING ROOFTOPS BLACK TEENYBOPPERS QUICK
   STEP BOUGALOO
VOLLEY DRUM BLAST   ARTILLERY FIRE

   black stepping drums
take over harlem tonight
            marcus garvey again alive
            banner fronts parade
            stopping main artery
            harlem   traffic
8TH AVENUE   7TH AVENUE
              125TH STREET
             the street the jew owns

and the parade starts
old cars   children in the street parading
winos and teenyboppers sidestepping & trailing
hired black band flailing out of tune
out of sight STRANGER IN PARADISE

stenciled bass drum of a boy passing
stuyvesant boys club brooklyn new york
& the worn tires of the 1957 buick station wagon
with no apparent function
than to go slow
& the goateed driver
              african garbed

                         his wife small children
                         posters in the back
           yes africans
                    & are they that wise?
                                   so un-american

to realize by racial ancestry
keen screaming genes & bloodcells
that 400 years has little truck
in the million years age span of man
poor peoples yes
                    black mass
                         since first slave
                                   indeed african

in dark noisey catch-as-catch-can parade
    with children street children
marching among and amok
white boots & hats high steppin majorettes /
a wino woman marching in middle
stiff legged in her stride
                    in her pride

    is it proud?   is it fun?   is it serious?   is it political?
is it
        ALL OF HARLEM STRAINED OUT OF WINDOWS
        STANDING ON FIRESCAPES
        STANDING ON SIDEWALKS   STANDING IN THE STREETS
        AS THE BUSES THE CABS THE TRAINS BOATS &
               PLANES HALT
        AS THE MARCHERS MARCH BACK TO AFRICA
                                   once more

The Last Set Saga of Blue Bobby Bland

For Pigeon

I

we could tell
yr head was buzzing
            a low key melody
as you sauntered onstage Apollo
yr canary-powdered face and
moot eyes
            bespake   hashish
            in stage door dressing rooms

you sang a mellow blues
hushed in the black neon
of yr custom-made hair   do
        who could have blown yr gyroscopic cool
save
        the soul sister
        who busted onstage
        to talk about her natural hair

yr marcel was pretty
next to her rugged *naturale*
but
    you were high
    and she was drunk /

II

BLUE BOBBY BLAND   KING OF THE BLUES
thrust to pop-sweat
by a sassy black sapphire /

one could say
you came back too many times
talkin shit
over the politics

41

but find the hesitation
in the blue depths of the orchestra
where a black voice   says
—*you aint got no soul!*

poor blue bobby
a headline star
on an uptight stage /
like the phalarope
you were one verse
too late

They Look This Way and Walk That Way
As Tribal as They Can Be Under the Law

sherman the barbecue man
famous former mayor of harlem
sittin   in his brand-new caddy
aunt jemama's hat on his head

in his barbecue parlor huge photos framed
shakin hands with rockefeller
standin next to truman

and in his chain   of barbecues
surround harlem no
porkchops / on the menu
remain

by day harlem blue sky
few industrial giants
or traffic cluster tourist
                          to clog the air
only the planes
                     high   jettison   smoke
               high   / mighty

possible public safety gesture
of administration / military / industry
cartel /   to fly as much   air
traffic over harlem
                          proper possible
in event of catastrophe
planes tumbling on welfare areas
        the last perimeter
                          black mass dispensable /

Sketches of Harlem

To Langston Hughes

It was Tiny's habit
to go down to THE GREAT WHITE WAY
without understanding the subway ride.

In the harlem morning
when sirens remind you
that you're burning—

Tiny Habit
Handy's broad
Hi-Hat Lounge 7th Avenue
in the morning rabbit
refuse mildew
with Negro for a color
and nothing for a hue.

Yin Years

I

New York City is a death festival
voluminous men death carriages /
cartels of internationally disposed people
dodder with bloat of water and sugar /
voluminous men
                  slow death ferment

Looking downtown / from Bowery roofs
the location marks
the balance of this city
to which all structures
of the city hall boys   fan
/ East by North

the magnificence of the Woolworth Building
will receive splendid disposition
with the first wave of holocaust—
                  overland they will come
    from Atlantic waters
across queens   brooklyn /   the harlem river
                  strange men will come

by bowery
the city casts voluminous light
on the caste of men
who patrol
upwards and downwards
their tree-lined corridor
to infinity

urban renewal
what will you do?
then   when you are too late /

when your young plastic saplings wither
& your fine printed reports
flutter in empty corridors
& grow yellow
                as the sun

by bowery
bloated men
voices of the disemboweled
yell ditties to each other
in endless short jostling games
that grow dangerous
by darkness
& cold light

jittery limbs
wine pressing skin
both ways
these are the short trunked people
whose trouser ends sweep the ground
& by morning light or red sundown
often limp on bare feet
pitiful & sober
faces shrunk by the racist sugar
                of sweet fruit drinks

bodies bludgeoned by
the red cross
holy ghost USA
port or amber fluid
falling
broken bottle limbs
gangrene
        of the corridor
man of epileptic gesture
                & embrace
where to be knocked down
is death in the face
where blood jumps

like crack bottle port 35 cent
Lou's wine Five Star Rhythm
North American port sherry & muscatel

II

by bowery
there are the elders
who speed by in their air-conditioned limousines
from City Hall or Wall Street
who appear
quite at odds
with old age
        sullen faces creased in frowns
      necks welded to shoulders
assholes abdomens bellies
locked up
crude collages
of toilet training
& panting desire
attention stature   antifornication
waxen men of destruction
      wan men
          held together by technology
          of machine & drugs
          oldsmobile & aspirins
          20th century plastics
there are men who call to god by plastic
decayed men who want to live forever
androids of science fiction
half men   half robots
          bing crosby
          owns a plastic liver
and is considered
a chic
old man /

plastic hearts veins glands kidneys dicks
modern men of America

47

dwarfed by racial sugar
   is there any mystery that the old men
   who would call down destruction
   do not & cannot live in the world /
it is the plastic men of technology
versus the natives of the land
the overfilled / overkill peoples
versus peoples who believe in their bodies
more than anything else
& who by necessity go hungry

III

by bowery
my dress is among the bums
the police cannot tell us apart
until I open the door to my loft
and disappear
   those who make friends
   with those who roam low
   in the streets
   reap reward
and by bowery
among bloated men
figurines of western death
I feel my blood go hot & cold
as theirs
from my many windows
I see them stagger / fall
stare pop bleary of the sun
their enemy
   their goddess of love defiled

I know their feeling
my blood remembers the wine
my cells have in their seven years construction
memory
of siren days / cartoon events

48

signifying a high kind of poison
a logical euthanasia /

by bowery   twilight falls
the caste of men
who by neon fluorescence
are not unlike one another /
everyone in America

A Documentary on Airplane Glue

I have seen the young Negroes & Puerto Ricans
sniffing and nodding in their slums
the young ones
old enough to afford only
the 25 cent Carbona or airplane glue
            the glue so paradoxically manufactured
for the assemblage of model airplanes /

I see the young boys 10   11   13 years
drawing nostrils to bottle   lip
and then staring woozily at their tenements
twice & thrice as old as their parents
or gazing at the monotonous pink dormitories
of the Housing Authority
set up so their fathers can remain at their meagre jobs
or their mothers on relief /

The pink buildings are tall
the tiny balsa wood planes the glue holds so well

never fly
            try to fly them & they'll break
            leave them lying around & they'll be broken
most of these boys
    have never been on a real plane
                    and never will
                    (unless they return to Puerto Rico
                    flying from poverty to poverty above the clouds /
                    . . . & *not* back to Africa)

& for a moment at least   sniffing the glue
can soar one above the pink & gray buildings /

the balsa wood planes are delicate
and crush easily
                    Sometimes I wonder how the effects of the glue
                    was discovered
Could it have been an eleven-year-old
bending so close to the tiny construction
piecing &   glueing   & piecing
gasping with slight exasperation
& then suddenly   wonderfully
                                    soaring
                    ultimately away /

---

across the big avenues
thru the trees
into the glen
flaming spears
from jungle rooftops

---

      white
      people
   strange customed
clan tongued clustering
    dark peopled ports   ages of europa
trains   boats   and planes
dionne warwick   says
              & in
          new york
     fluid dark causeways
    gangplanked streets
  eerie lights of darkness

clustering natives
          tightly bundled
       europeans of the 400 millennial
                     race war
      fighting peoples of clans & kabalas
axed   gunshot ancestors
stained blood fibers   of cellular centuries
some baked some fried
          some burned
              some blue

Elvin Jones Gretsch Freak

Coltrane at the Half Note

To Elvin Jones/tub man of
the John Coltrane Quartet.
GRETSCH is outstanding on
his bass drum that faces the
audience at the Half Note,
Spring Street, New York City.

gretsch love
gretsch hate
gretsch mother   father fuck
fuck gretsch

The Half Note should be
a basement cafe like the "A" train
Jazz /   drums of gretsch
on the fastest and least stopping
transportation scene in NYC
subways are for gretsch
"A" train long as a long city block
the tenements of the underground rails
west 4th
34th   42nd   125th
farther down in the reverse
                                    local at west 4th
waterfront   warehouse   truck / produce   vacant
the half note
                    our city fathers keep us on the right track
zones /   ozone
                    fumes of tracks   / smokestacks

The Half Note
westside truck exhaust and spent breath
of Holland Tunnel   exhaust   soot darkness jazz
speeding cars   noisy /   noiseless
speeding gretsch   tremulous gretsch
Elvin Jones the man behind the pussy

52

four men love on a stage
the loud orgy
gretsch trembles and titters
                    gretsch is love
                    gretsch is love
                    gretsch is love

Elvin's drum ensemble the aggressive cunt
the feminine mystique
cymbals tinny clitoris   resounding
lips snares flanked /   encircling
thumping foot drum peter rabbit the fuck   take
this   and take   that
elvin behind the uterus of his sticks
the mad embryo
panting sweat-dripping embryo
misshapen /   hunched
Coltrane sane / cock   the forceps
the fox and the hare
the chase
screaming and thumping
traffic of music on Spring Street
'Trane says to young apprentice Ron Ferral "fill in the solids,
get it while it's hot and comely;   Elvin fucks almost as good
as his Mama."
The Half Note is as packed as   rush hour on 42nd & 8th
"A" train territory
Coltrane is off with a hoot
directed supine
nowhere in generalness
into the din and the death
between   bar and tables   reds silver glass molten mass shout
tobacco fumes across the boardwalk
                    (coney island is the "D" train change
                    at west 4th if you want it)
Coltrane steps the catwalk
                    elvin jones drums gretsch
                    gretsch shimmy and shout
elvin drums a 1939 ford

99 pushing miles per hour /   shoving barefoot driver
                    in the heats /

Coltrane /   Jones
riffing   face to face
instrument charge
            stools to kneecap
many faceted rhythm structure   to   tomahawk
gretsch rocks n rolls   gretsch rattles
fuck gretsch /
                we know so well strident drums
                children singing death songs   / war
                tenor and soprano   high
tenor soar /   flux of drums   chasing
        keen inviolate   blue
the model "T" ford & air hammer
                Holland tunnel
                "Avenue of the Americas"
                cobbled stones /   din of rubber
                of tin
to the truck graveyard
lineup of Boston Blackie nights /   deserted
right here model "T" & tomahawk
                sometimes late in silent din of night
                I hear
                bagpipes /   death march
                music of ago /   kennedy

gretsch   gretsch tune optical color-jumping gretsch
    Elvin's F-86 Sabre jet / remember Korea / Horace Silver
    the fine smooth jackets the colored boys brought back
    from the far east with "U.S. Air Force" a map of Japan
        blazing the back   —a forgotten flame

Elvin tom-tomming
bassing the chest   "E" / gretsch   "J" / gretsch
                clashing metal mad
                tin frantic road of roaring / gretsch
                roar

peck morrison
the *bass* player
told me once about a drum set
with a central anchor /   every drum connected
      unable to jump or sway
      drums like the cockpit of a TXF spy plane
      ejaculator seat and all
                    (call up brubecks joe dodge, al hirt
                    lester lanin et al)

pilot conflict
and the man elvin behind the baptismal tubs
that leap like cannons   to the slashing sound of knives
black elvin knows so well
the knives the *Daily News* displays along with the photo
of a grinning award-winning cop
the kind of knives elvin talks about
downtown by the water
and uptown
near the park.

Do Nothing till You Hear from Me

For Langston Hughes

i arrive   / Langston
the new york times told me when to come
but i attended your funeral
late
by habit of colored folk
and didnt miss a thing

you lie on saint nicholas avenue
between the black ghetto & sugar hill
where slick black limousines await yr body
for the final haul
from neutral santa claus avenue
harlem usa

you are dressed sharp & dark as death
yr cowlick is smooth
like the negro gentleman
in the ebony whiskey ads /
gone is yr puff of face
yr paunch of chest
tho   yr lips are fuller now
especially
on the side
where hazard had you
                    a cigarette /

two sisters
          felines of egypt
vigil yr dead body
one is dressed in a bean picker's brown
the other is an erstwhile gown
of the harlem renaissance /
they chatter

like all the sapphires
of Kingfish's harem /
                    old sisters
                        old relations

in writing the fine details
of yr last production
you would have the black sapphires / there
guardians of yr coffin
                    yr argosy
                        in life & death
the last time blues /
                with no hesitations . . .

                        day of the vernal winds / 1967

57

Jocko for Music and Dance

There was a dance called the "bop"
and there was also a dance we used to do in the street
with our walk
talk of diddy-bops   talk of bopping
        the charismatic cobra sway of head and vertebrae
        the angle step of lame feet /
peaked caps   tightly rolled stetsons
stingy brims flat and tilted like the earth's orbit

sometimes Jocko is the only person I know
the only person from my past who offers memory
        without propaganda

let me speak of tribal ritual & dance
let me declare Jocko my atavistic purveyor of tribal tunes
        and gossip—

        the medicine man who strings the tendons of memory incarnate

Jocko hustles wine & compoz . . . duds for the head
and plays James Brown back to back

Jocko is in front of Harlem Hospital
brown wrapping paper spread on propped up suitcase
selling to all who will listen
dream twigs   crushed leaves   liver-lips   neckbones prime mojo
—contraband from the ghetto
                        up rocket ship
                        and away

Harlem Xmas

For Langston Hughes

by winters
        summer festivals subside
cold winds cross the wide boulevards
war on poverty
       having spent herself on summer fun
retreats like a vanguard whore

the children begin to dance
                          again
the karate
successor to the bougaloo

cold druid seasons
approximate the age
       huge fires of midwinter
       or the whiskey-fires   mid-belly
       los indios called firewater
dont burn like sun
or sit
       on cold stoops /

bop down
where you see
            the war on poverty
        a traveling
                minstrel show

Louisiana Weekly

Summer, 1967

Caravan

1

along the speeding highways
southern stars churn / quiet white light
graves unincorporated
                    is the only insurance

here
   i would study
     the origins of the sisters
find
the genius of american dance
       sitting on the lips
       of a toothless shack

2

& below
     many many little pickaninnies cry
          for the nation
drooning like oriental wiseman /
   koolaid
       may ease the pain
but the music of the race
will suffice
the sleepy hamlets

What Bert Say

when i come to a new town
first i get with the town
then i find the people
if the town dont sit right
then i
split

A Coltrane Memorial

my first day in new orleans
                home-house of jass
coltrane dead
                in my dreams
among marching creoles
among marching blacks
                bojangling jass parade
in *le quartier*
as a resident of a black theatre thru southland
i laid upon carver's grave   lingered in his laboratory
                                                in tuskegee
i kissed Laly   an ancestor
                                of booker t.
she wore her hair afro
& played coltrane all night   slow

where the southern cross
the yellow dog

long caravan speeding thru alabama
then georgia red clay
black theatre of an albany backwood church
and then
        the long convoy stretch to new "o"
to find coltrane dead
amid the rubble
of newark negroes

i would want my favorite things
in summertime ritual
have coltrane
        the medicine man
of my ancestral journeys
towards my favorite moments

energy dies
energy dies
        tumult or riots
                die
    the way of escape
    the underground rails
        the trains
the freight   train
            coltrane
          cargo of fate
    as we ride on
    up
      the way

Burgundy Street

four stories high
i viz both waterways of new o
the mississippi crescents devil horns
as lake ponchartrain shimmies to the ancient fires along her shores
both bring the breezes
from the gulf of mexico or usa proper
to this point
where all
            empties out

a bourbon street jiggle
by sundown or sunrise
will uncover legions of white women
shouting   arms high
bellyrollin   and   ahumpin   to public climax
amid the consumption of light

walk the track
step back
emperors line motel balconies
toasting the din
toasting the death

round the corner
the old black jassmen are preserved in a hall
waiting for the saints
to come amarching in
& riot

i live in *vieux carré*
the old quarter of the french
where the blacks line the narrow arcades
drinking regal beer /

                    they await the late
                            marie   laveau   the vodun queen
                                            to come on in
            but the train from congo square
                                    is lost

riot sale

in the gun shop again . . .
a friday afterwork crowd
weekend rush
all white folks solemn
a reverent ceremony
held in hushed voice
the range / velocity of projectile / size of prospective wound
("bring it back and we'll give you your money")
all customers cluster gun counter
in church
a laughing cop in attendance
(his gun the biggest anyone could ever pray for)
                            —aint nobody interesting in fishing anymore
no one wants a rifle
like they intend to hunt game
this is not the time
                    nor the age
                            for pretense

Ruckus Poem

I

THE POLICE PROTECT THE STORES
THE POLICE PROTECT THE STORES
GOOD GOD IN SMOKE CRY FOR THE GOODS
GOD THE PEOPLE IN FRONT OF THE STORES
FIRE THE GUNS IN FRONT OF THE STORES
POLICE PROTECTION
POLICE PROTECTION
                    INSURRECTION   INSURRECTION /
THE POLICE PROTECT   THE WHEEL OF FORTUNE
DEATH IN THE FACE   SPIN   PICK A NUMBER
BY FULL MOON   SATURDAY NIGHT
OF SATURN   OF SATURN   O SATURN   MY SATURN
O MY GOD!
A GANG OF MONKEYS HAVE SURROUNDED THE SHOPPING CENTER
THE ARE CARRYING OFF THE TELEVISIONS!
DONT WORRY LUCY & DESI & CHET & OZZIE & FLINTSTONES
BLAM LAM LAM

MACHINE GUN FIRE POWER VIETNAM VETERANS CHARGE
        LAUNDROMAT
MUSTER AT THEOLOGICAL BANK   WITH THE FLAG ON TOP

CITY CIVIL WAR
BETTER BELIEVE IT   BETTER BELIEVE IT
VIETNAM OUTSIDE THE PICTURE WINDOW
100 YEARS AGO BLACK TROOPS TURNED THE TIDE
AGAINST THE STATES
PRESENT GUN TENSE SHOOT 100 YEARS IN BLACK CHROMOSOMES /
AINT NO BOMBS FALLING FROM PLANES
NEVER NO FOREIGNERS CAUSING RUCKUS ON OUR TURF
BUT O LORD   WHERE DID THOSE NIGGERS COME FROM
O SAMBO THE MAN-EATER

O SAMBO SO TERRIBLE   SO TERRIBLE
OUR CHILDREN WOULD HAVE TO BELIEVE HIM
A BOY EATING WATERMELON IN THE GARDEN OF MYTH
WITH SHANGO THE MAN-EATER
SAMBO   THE MAN-EATER
SAMBO   THE MAN-EATER
THE KIND OF NIGGER   YOU CANT DO NOTHING WITH
THE CRAZY NIGGER   / *O SHANGO!*

II

ENTIRE REGIMENT OF VIETNAM REGULARS PINNED DOWN
BY THE MIGHTY BLACKSTONE RANGERS
TEENYBOPPERS FROM CITIES OF WIND

CREATE YR OWN JOBS
CREMATE SELF-DETERMINATION IN THE 20TH CENTURY
LIKE A NATION   LIKE ANY OTHER NATION   ANY NOTION
MAY AS WELL DO THIS OR THAT
INTEGRATE OR SEGREBURN

III

BURN SIEGE   RIOT AND RUCKUS
BOOD RUCKUS BLOOD RUCKUS
NIGGERSNIPERFIRE
NIGGERSNIPERFIRE
BLACK FLAG   BLACKBOMBS   BLACKBOMBS
THEYBOMB   THEYBOMB   NAPALM   NAY BOMB
NAYBOMB
NAY BOMB
    NIGGERFIREBOMB

SHATTERED   SHATTERED   SHATTERED
DREAM SHATTERED   GLASS SHATTERED
GLASS IN FRONT OF PROTECTED DREAM
PROTECT   DREAM   SHATTER   GLASS

SHARDS   GLASS SHARDS   SIRENS
FIRE DEMONS
GUTTED STOOPS   GUTTED WINDOWS
SMOKE ARSON NIGGERS   OUR SONS   OUR BOYS   OUR SONS
SHOOT THEM ARSONS   SHOOT THEM IN THE BACKS
OUR SONS IN THE MAN'S BACK
MY BOYS   MY BOYS   MY BOYS   DEPLOY
1000 OF MY BOYS   DEPLOY OUR SONS   DEATH
ON THEIR FACES SEARCH AND SEIZE   SEARCH AND SEIZE
THE NATIONAL GOD
OUR GUARD   O GOD DEPLOY   OUR GUARD
OUR NATIONAL NOTIONAL GOD
KEEP THE FAITH
SEARCH AND DESTROY
THE DESTROYERS DEATH /

IV

NEGRO MEANS DEAD BODY
NEGRO MEANS DEAD BODY
NEGRO MEANS DEAD
ETCHED IN SHANGO RED
BLACK FIRENESS *BLACK FIRENESS*
INTERNECINE STOMP
DOWN BROADWAY
DOWN FUNKY BROADWAY
DOWN FUNKY FUNKY BROADWAY
KINK KONG SNATCHES OUT THE LIGHT
KING KONG BOPS DOWN TIMES SQUARE

                              FUNKY BROADWAY

THEY GOT ROI they got roi   they got roi
stomped him good
said he had two loaded 32s   2 32s
roi wasnt ready   roi wasnt ready
he could at least have had some 45s some TOMMY GUNS some TANKS
but who's ready for broadway when she gets funky

70

who's gonna love her then
aint nothing to it
aint nothing to it
dont tell that to the white folks tho
might kill them to know
                    aint nothing to it
what am i living for
if not for you
funky funky Broadway & my father KING KONG
lord he was no good   *lord* he was no good

in williams

in williams
i would drink all 1100 springs of texas
by way of the pearl beer company

in *le quartier*
williams down n dirty bar & grill
chickens dance on concrete floors
as the sparrow flies friday night
jax n dixie regal & falstaff lager
local beer demons fix black lips

twin partners spar
yogi trousers bend the knees
inside that other body
shirttails fly in moon winds
charity hospital chloroform wall paper
glows   fire & water talisman
                              (*are you eligible?*)

crescent city beelzebub horns
guide prowl cars below sea level
thru gulf of mexico nights

off bourbon street
the jass musicians are preserved
in a hall
old granddad stands sentry
in alabaster /

en la calle burgundy
black scarecrows surrender
when the light of tony's superette / fails

piccolo say
thread the needle
we gonna do it

cat tails bump n grind
puppet pelvis strings
belly rein
high in hand
this i can do
that i cannot
the elderly gentleman laughs
all the pictures off the wall /

razors in the wind
thread the needle
thread the needle
we gonna do it

The Murals of the Stations

for marilyn

the mural of the train station
tells of pain and passion
between here and acapulco
stateside the other traveler
walks in danger
southside of the train.

at commencement /   of the last jass funeral
our second line procession down
ramparts n dumaine
may receive a visitation
nuns in flying saucers
coming down over our dancing umbrellas

sixteen vestal virgins headlined
the veterans of foreign wars parade
the crowd called out for more

women who belong to no men
worldwide lock up jelly between the thighs
babies crying in walls of womb

jefferson parish police jury legend has it
1400 embryos found in the walls
of a french quarter nunnery

in new o
highways have run
the black nun voodoo dancers
across the river
                  to algiers

in new o
old black men
live hundreds of years

they drink swamp water
mixed with goofer dust
& eat hardshelled ancestors
from the sea
that look like roaches

Riot / Shout Laugh & Talk

supermarket   burning womb
women who belong to no men
in pyres of burning flesh
machine gun bullets thru six-floor windows
picture window televisions coming in for the kill
vomiting fire   snakes and dead babies
nuns land in flying saucers
red crosses on top

On the Town

1

Chas. Self. young black poet from LSU
drives big old buik
is hunched in the left vector /
wheeling hot rod driver
fast takeoffs
down louisiana streets
sensation of hurtling in a big heavy car
four door

2

they take me to the red door
where they have natural-haired go-go girls
they sit on the mini stage
and dont smile between numbers
they drink pop   smoke   and chew gum
(paraphernalia of many a trade)
but when the music plays
they shake like a hot bitch on the strip
they do EVERYTHING and make it look good
aint nothin to it
tune over
they sit down
and frown /
outside the red door
a red woman is painted the length
she is smiling

3

now this is the cafe my man from philly digs
tinkling laughter   mellow conversation   tasteful lighting
a sequined universe / of ceiling space   stars sprinkled on black
this is where we get drunk

as i'm dipping in the 1100 springs of the pearl beer company
chas. self wants to fight philly cause he talked about his ma
felix say
you dont play the dozens self? /
laughing can douse fire like water

4

we pass the robin hood hotel on two wheels
green forest fluorescent light douses the porch
green tinted company
weird
as if a play were going on   (upon a balcony)
we park and pass it again
two united allied truckers in uniform abide porch
pass them rows of rooms
and carpet leads to all red
O Shango

5

right next to robin hood
an invisible door   leads to a lair
—every broad in here is a prostitute / self say
we twine to table
four of us take positions   facing the floor
the entire bar /   the show, philly says, we are here
watching a show
why dont we leave them alone to their misery?
good question / why dont we leave ourselves alone to our own
private misery?   felix   he laugh.
self opponent / i'm an artist   i observe people
i got lots of good character studies out of this place
long black lanky man   does the jig /   james brown is in a cold sweat
no one plays either of them mind   cept philly
are we here to watch them like in a zoo?
black type   grotesque in black light
tall wigged whores   fat man & fat mama
coincidence

we were asked for matches   joked and jostled like brothers
release the pain of reconnection
to find philly & self both   fingerpoppin rather angrily
to the hot rhythm n blues /

The Louisiana Weekly #4

    a phone duet over the radio
the night
we got our leading lady out of jail
they were talkin   about handling niggers
the white folks was
one suggestion:
                in event of a riot
                to flood the canals in the negro section /
they probably got the idea
from the last flood /
when the big department stores were threatened
when they had to blow the industrial canal
                                to siphon some water off
happened to be right near black town the bombs fell
many blacks drowned
others were ferried by private boats
                        for a fee
many blacks drowned
                    the city
            never did get
        all the names

The Murals of the Terminals

O the terminals and waiting stations of america
monster depots
for the mass movement of populations
                    to and fro

for the people   for my people
ride the land
                by car   by highway   by sealed beam headlight
you will not know one place
from the other

thunder over the airports
floods along the rails   this is
new orleans
home house of jass

In New O

all the street cleaners wear
orange tee shirts   green bush khakis & sneakers
they are
remarkably
uniformly
thin

shaking
rattling
& rolling their carts
a dragon broom sticking out

or they
trot along   (like basketball players)
side the cantering truck
churning cauldrons of debris

a sundown procession
down the spanish arcades

Fork of the West River
and Beyond

1966–1969

once in love with
always in love with
never in love with
amy

she wanted to dance
                  that is all
and she danced
like a congolese dervish
late in silent din of night
in front
          of the jukebox
alone in her room
alone
        in silent din
of the west river
                    moving

The Fork of the West River

for amy

introit
a fast cab along the west river
a soul brother who wheels
& deals the passing gear
in the mash-potato blood cells of his foots /
voom   voom /   blam-lam
                    musical mad highways
                    west river seaweed stinking
                    wafts of funk jersey blows blues
                                far a-shore
and o
        look see what they did to palisades!
        all lights   all river sheen   no ferry cross
cars by night speed race the stars
white neon bulbs loom lanes of highway
insects inside arches of light speed
concentric into the distance
into the dust
            swirls   cycles of lights
            that challenge the stars
on telstar nights   satellites cast
the only heavenly lights we can see

o which ones are bell telephone asteroids?
o where are the orbs of fairy tales
in the sky / ?

AT THE WORLDS PREMIER OF "SEVEN YEAR ITCH"
MARILYN MONROE SMOKED DMT WITH TOM EWELL
AND HER GOWN FLEW OVER HER HEAD

the river spirits are good people
along the west river
where thru rank fumes we visit
the ancestral rooms of our minds /
we are well supplied with fresh bread

84

and the latest vision from the kabala
and we will venture out of our rooms
to vision murder & mandalas in the streets

saga proper
6am on the parkway of the cathedrals
we are craving dessert
a soggy bundle below a park bench
yells for help
and no one pays her no mind /
aqui se habla espanol
THEY BEAT ME THEY MUGGED ME   please a cop
aminata telephones the police
then cradles the dent-headed lady
in her arms
so we stay for a cop
those guys who like keystone and legend
are never around when you need them /

we wait too long
i tell you
you should have screamed over the phone
A WOMAN HAS BEEN MAIMED BEHEADED DISMEMBERED
        AND PULVERIZED
IN FRONT OF COLUMBIA UNIVERSITY
then immediately
a convoy of red strobe screaming police cars
ambulances & black *Daily News* sedans
moving bedlam towards the scene /

but it is 6am this sleepy hamlet
as our lady's head flattens the concrete
a casual pedestrian curbs a dog

the cops are here
they look at our lady
O NO NOT HER AGAIN
they tell you to leave her alone

then they call the ambulance /
they repair to their nervous dog prowl car
only to have to get out angry
they want you to leave her alone
he taps you with his report
authority of the law
passed thru impartial tools /

a bewildered ambulance trolls thru
the empty streets / stops
knickerbocker hospital
the soul brother nurses aide
calls our lady soul sister
they buck her up with smelling salts of ammonia
buck her in the wagon
brace her up
tie her down
and take off

you say
you say
aminata
they treat her like shit
you are
exactly right

you want to wash your hands now
for dessert you wipe yr hands on the napkins
now breakfast is necessary
a new fortification   a new start
you bolt pancakes and lots of butter
you leave me and run home
to throw up
to collect thru defecation

our heads are never the same
once we leave our house
as when we return

I

O these days of waking and falling
                asleep
run out to peek the towers
               that surround—
watchdogs   in art nouveau trimmings /
the buildings are alive
they speak to the other shore
                  along the west river

O these days of ennui & malaise
of mayhem & murder
             in every street /
         look in any window
fear of the night riders
hope for the vigilantes
             in every stone-encased block
         trappings of the druids
        whispers of gothic murders

ask the towers
the abandoned bell crypts on high
or the balustrados / lining the rooftops
they have seen all
they are the first to get the news
            look in any window

i wd say—hey!
         to the palisades
the other side of the great hudson
the commencement of america proper
and chart a route by wind tide clear across to pacifica
and when i turn around VIZ
           the end of america / end of the land

          thru manhattan
                    sights

          II

O the broadway subway train
                              travels quickly thru
                                        these parts
                    to rear above ground
                    like a giant sex star
to say hello
                    to the girls at Barnard

the dracula organ crescendos
amidst the cathedrals of higher education
          that line this morningside
the valiant soldiers of the battle of Harlem Heights
are buried beneath
                    the ebb of towers
                              the listing spires!

O look for the western sky changing
          the no horizon you see
                    above the roof towers

the river spirits are good people
                    along the west river

but there is that law
                    of diminishing returns
          as we venture inland
          past the college of the kings /

          III

those midnight tappings on the windowpanes
reach forth many arms
the curtains fly

silently
to other entities than the wind alone
the rustlings of the courtyards
the eyes of the windows
the arms of the gothic spires
                    will embrace you in sleep
                    like a lover

if your ancestors
are to drag dead bodies thru yr room
do question them closely

o man the darkness
    man the tides
along the ecclesiastical towers of
west river on high /

Fork of the West River (19)

To the late Shorty Long

   the last of a long return   home
a cat on the stairway   follows me thru my door
a solution
the fellow inhabitation of space   by two creatures
o how i remember my former cats   like loves
how i wd woo them
throw them around
forget their meals
anomalies never worked out
no conclusion   only withdrawal
like an army   win or lose
a logical army
entropy of all matter
    like logjam   of the mind

mark a return
from the fork of the west river
far uptown where the university sprawls its multi people
where the ennui of populace   and the malaise of persons
is paramount
like the ecclesiastical towers
that line the causeways
of the hudson river /

first it was love on the lower east side
by exercise upon early rising
the perfumed lady upon my bed
a witness before a tomb
audience to the cosmic gesturing /
to conclude the supplications
to fall beside bathsheba
smell the musk of body scent
warm and thick congestion at the function
before the junction

your mound of venus
groundswells   sweet & full
i churn and twist that gyroscopic top
to the conclusion of that act
and the beginnings
of the junction
and before us / in between us
is no unction for the worldwide control of birth
only that fluid
warm & lubricant cycles true secretion
                            in its own time
hail the arch flowing wide legs
moving high along the body-ruba
to challenge the shoulder span
the supine eyes
rising
out of the forehead

volcanic current connects
coaxial cables of body contortion
towards acme of all

Pigeon and Me (7)

then it is to west river by dawn light
  along the rivers phalanxes of automobiles
traveling without sleep
into the list of afternoon
the waking into the waning sun
leap down to the river, lovers!
splash the water
reap the sun
in the plum blues
hovering atop jersey factories
that final plunge into night
what we have been saving for
and o yes
we must make palisades one night
this millennium!

Fork of the West River (5)

from my windows
i hear the rain of the water hydrants
seems like water brings the breezes
seems like nighttime brings the breezes

by summer-in-the-city days
i walk huge dust storms
along the popular avenues
looking for my son

sometimes i walk uptown
facing the palisades from across the great hudson
where the cathedrals of higher education loom high
against the sky

sometimes i walk thru central park
and find
that as we near the ghetto
the park becomes a mountain
which we must overcome
for a good fish sandwich

Rock n Rolling w/ the Champion Celts

To Martha

its all the same
    all the same

young girls in spring
        vernal skies

like nature apropos

a snow falls
yet the light
you can see

the brightness calls
—hold on i'm coming

its all the same

dimpled smiles of long haired young

oldening feeling
causal relation w /
women of old feelings /
to understand is to love

all the way
apotheosis of goddess / white
graves & tombs

why not the best!
cream of karma's end

it may be the same day
     again & again

beauty in me life
walk clean w / chuck berry
high school days
& after   noon /

Time Zone Poem

For Cal

I

by winters
you find the sun down
in the other river
as the sky plays the hesitation blues
the last time death
of sun down

twilight   the masses
from harlem to lower east side
the space
of a nation

grey winds of night fire
stroke the polluted city
sealed beam headlights
astral green faces
illume
the canary moon
as it walks

twilight the masses

II

walking in the panels of the sun
midtown streets
                    are paved with gold
concrete slabs appear silver bullion

along the fifth avenue
garbage cans
stand like golden sentry
block by block /

by daze
there is a watchtower

on every street corner
a drunken old lady
of the kingdom
standing in the alley
of the puritan hotel
screams AWAKE!
as the cops chase
                    KING KONG
                              thru the streets
                              in broad daylight

every morning
i go and see
the white women
in the glass windows /
i have heard
they often
appear nude
to huge crowds

for lunch
i go
to the grand jury
bar and grill
and discotheque
with the war lords
in zigzag vinyl raincoats

and· when
the airraid jiggle
occurs at noon
i duck underground
to get high
with Shango

Walking in the panels
of the sun
the black sapphires
hang out like stars
on the geode transistors

of our nations
they scream
hot black jelly roll
they predict
the hunters
will be captured
by their game /

o that i wd heed
the young singers
as they signal
the seasons
over the radio

by the noontide melancholy
sandstorms drive the buses
cars scatter
every which way
like a runaway tribe
electric dinosaurs
howl in & out of tunnels
and run amok
on the underground rails

in the danny boy saloon
(a whiskey warehouse
with wholesale prices)
i wd stalk to stand
with all the balding
young men who want to go naked
we toast
the burns detectives
who protect
the white women
who stand
in the glass casement
windows
            we sing /
    we drink what they give us

we take it like it is
we take what is proffered
we drink what they give us

III

twilight the masses
from harlem
to lower east side

the clouds will suggest
how fast we move
the moon
will walk us
to death /
i stare into cars
i count the cops
i watch the sky
                    look in any window

i move towards
the low vector
of this island
a jericho walk by dawn
down the laugh house of Shango

towards the old colonial section
where the hearth burns
in the fire
where
the love fascist chant
as werewolves sink fangs
into flesh

signs say
      LIQUOR   DRUGS   PEOPLE   GET HIGH
get   get   good god good   god

o let the streets look like cartoons again!

mainly
i drink my phisohex wine
and stroll
along the crowded thoroughfares
where traffic jags
and neon flicks
and an occasional song
comes from nowhere

sometimes
i move staccato fast
and scream with the sirens
as manhole covers explode
in the night

electric guitars
machine gun
over the sonar winds
each blast as long
as a cigarette

walking in the panels
of the red sundown
the black sapphires
trance sisters
scream at me
all night long

by full moon
we walk together
like lovers holding
hand on beam /
by the light
of the saturn sun
i wd try to be / porkchop & beautiful / for
there is blue funk
in the near
unknown

Pentecostal Sunday / A Song of Power
(it aint the father
it aint the son
its the holy ghost
yall)

for willie and melba

1

the boys from ancient philadelphia
                    calling.
    our Lady of Guadalupe
    Saint Martin de Porres
    Saint Expedite
        do it now!

he was cripple in the aisle
walking with a cane
the preacher broke up his cane
the preacher spit fire on the man
the man burn up
the sisters sing
the organ play
the man dance in the aisle
    HOW MANY PEOPLE HERE SAW GOD!
    LIFT THIS MAN UP OFF HIS CANE

pentecostal sunday
north africa to rome
en route a donkey a coffin
with in
    the original christian church
    the original christian
    ritual
    the holy ghost
    the holy ghost
        within the feel in the dance
        within the spirit in the dance

in getting of spirit
in body of dancer

in the sweat gyre head falling off
heat fire body sweat
power of the atom
grows a breast back on in Spanish Harlem
power to set the devil
power to handle the snakes
power to be what you want to be
spirits
    on the temple floor
    writhing and screaming
    jumping and shouting
    getting happy
            they have come
            doing the jackleg and bougaloo
fear no fear
fear no fear
fear no fear
        fear no fear
                in the original christian ritual
                north africa and reverend ike
                glory glory
                        he say
                put your hand on the radio
                repeat after me
        IT COST MONEY TO BE ON THE AIR
        TO BRING THIS MESSAGE TO YOU BUT
        EVERYBODY GOT SOMETHING AND
        IT TOOK SACRIFICE TO GET IT

        2

yusef rahman say
yeah
        them preachers talkin bout the real thing
        aint nothing like the real thing
        when reverend ike say put god on the spot

102

he's saying put yourself   yusef on the spot
when you got trouble
he'll surely get you out.

the ritual original
in the black storefront temple
drum organ guitar cricket swish of tambourine
glory
glory
glory
bid the preacher to teach
cause the shit is deep

pentecostal preacher
man of god
strong man of tongue of heart
ptah of egypt lay source to Osiris
corn in the earth hearth
next to the water
the river spirits are good people
the crossing over
wash basin / wooden raft
take me over
dance upon delta
isis
morning
do it now!

Thelonius
Sphere
Monk

loud niggers talkin more than shit
the blue monk swirling rainbows
in count basies lounge
with his people he dont show up late /
big tooth smile
homeboy home again
amber lights orchestras bassoons and lady sopranos
in chorus in cocaine johns slow motion zen space
face of the count over the dead piccolo
iridescent suit in day-glo shimmer
with the music and the space white saddle shoes
skip in space off and on the pedals
chandelier ring on the trill pinky
talmud cap bopping bebop beard

he lay in de cut
he dont talk loud
but he talk that talk
just the same

blue monk
on the island of the blue dolphins
all over the bronx
and upper manhattan
showing up
by the dozens

my man knows
he knows
when he knows /

letters from mama
the calling
come home son
before I die

Love Factory Incarnation Blues

For the women who walk the street
and have nowhere to go

body commodity
like old times
walking the street
feet like rats
plague thee down
o beauteous body
of the first cartel
international freight
locked to hold in ship
long limbed outwards
to eat shit die in own
locked with neighbor
to eat shit to eat death

o look how beauty full she is
teeth like horses
back and buttocks the same way
on lenox avenue
surplus commodity body
sold to lack
what is missing
love of body
suck the titty
mammy transformed
to lover
mount mammy
let her show thou
thee jelly roll
work for lack
of merchandise
on marketplace
be it love of mamma
or love of love
in the sexual body commodity
soft big lips

to wrap around
what that pure god lost
and never got back

burst love
in ritual of blood
     partake of the body
     partake of the blood
relive
thru time and space
a death of spirit
in name of a man /

a ritual of blood
drunk upon the altar
hermaphrodite
in black in white
crossed
double-crossed
speak out to thee
o lord
the beauty of our ways
the folly of the wise
set in fancy rooms

women of the night
women of the street
our fem spirit
abominated
for lack of bread and wine
and spiritual body to love
walk pure limbs
long as mating would allow
supple
big breasted and buttocked
like the anthropoids say
this is my love
this is my love
to have
and to
hold

Reverend King / Elijah Too / El Malik / M.L.K.

1

we were in the apollo
at the gospel show
james cleveland broke down
over the lords prayer
sobs of women
exploding all around
echoing
in the blue shell
of the black theatre /
the mighty clouds of joy
moaned and groaned
beat their chests
and grimaced
like the devil—
the only ritual
we knew
in those long days

2

steel gates peeled
from their storefronts locks
jaws
in concrete tenement
blooms
steel flowers /

3

and the
death ceremonies of fire
across the nation /
fires that cannot be put out

cremation
of king
and all his kind
going with him
crossing over
to the other
side

4

a secret of the blood
across the nation
synchronize
glass bombs
fossil fuel fires
metal fatigue
atomic weight
squared
steel girders strangled to death
lay thee down
bullets flying into the night
tracing arc's glow
televisions
getting up and walking
out of grey credit factories
best liquor in the world
flowing down sewers
storefront glaciers
raped by black mobs
breaking
steel gaged chastity belts
thru the hymen
into the goods
o so good
hot and comely
hot
o god good
bloods

5

brother
you my boy
if anybody fuck with you
they got to fuck with me
we are down together
if they get you
they got to get me
too

6

mountain high
valley low
he walked up the mountain
he walked
he walked
he was gone
already
gone.

no death in vanity
no death in vanity
like adonis
no death in vain
what did he have to do
to make him
so black
so blue

he tuned his tongue
did the holy roll
did the holy roll
he tuned his tongue
he sang that song
of far away of glory
of

glory
glory
he sang that song
of glory

7

reverend king say
wonderful   wonderful
how is everybody?
wonderful
wonderful
to the children
of a mississippi parish
they are the wards
they are the words
they remain

wonderful
wonderful

Night Driver

1

thru city compartments
in red light
lane between planets
check out the river
its flowing
cant stop

blackbirds   ride the icebergs
faster than they can fly
winter trees shriek out
sap flowing slow

harlem moving
several arcs in the roadway spin
and then down the embankment
all the symbols we need
fall out in the street

2

the feudal doll is screaming bout
one dollar and thirty five cent
james brown is dealing in black electricity
if you love me baby
baby baby baby

call a ritual to mass
sit down to the table
make the word flash
an advent of liquids
weights and measures
falling vessels in space
into the faces of desolate gods

Egyptian Book of the Dead

pharisees come bloom
water eddys the twilight air
blue for music
red for fire
look out along the rooftops
ancient cities pop up
old testaments
tribes muster at grey street corners
sparks of cigarettes gleam the glass arcades
wine bottles libate the sidewalk
no more
the wine from palms
no more
the beer from bananas
but
easy now
easy
this night will turn you on /

where
death is a beautiful thing
done in the right way
and to die
tonight
in the street
on the radio
in the fire
will fare us well

we who are nothing
to the incarnate computers
save factors on a graph
we who are nothing
rescued by love
we cannot fathom
walk jaded neon jewelry

twinkling
twinkling
so delicate to the touch
to fall down
in a blaze of trumpets
in a blossom of fire
we
are from a place far off

———————

de bar room was full of black men
coo cooing in each others ears
some sapphire
was screaming some shit
all de way from detroit
torpedo heads
lips as lank
as the flap of an arm
in gesture
the flow of upturned glasses
flashing white gin
into de basket

trance oriental
horace silver
song for my father
in a pyramid set
master
of de temple
in a pyramid set
cairo stockholm hong kong
philadelphia paris morocco
harlem jass
charka drums
sticks beat concrete
brass screams crack the walls /

the black boy
was ragged in white
his sky
all upside his head
bopping
into the garden of music
looking for isis /

_____

tenor roars
obbligato
laughin like a drunken woman
walk up the stairs
scream
and then fall back   down
again

114

chant chant sheet glass windows
glaciers of upper kingdom
stark screams shatter glass
runs the tracks under trees of lightning
hung out over red trailers
diminishing
into civilization
ciditty

sax man
of the baronette
he relax
in the blue contours
of your soul

amber glows
golden wheels of fire
yellow vapor rises in the room
and slips thru the door
the sequined man shimmers across the floor
holding an ax between his teeth
he's fucking with the walls of the void
mama said
the crowd responded:
YOU AINT NOTHING BUT THE OLD TESTAMENT!

city of the people
leaves of the grass
e-lectronic shimmy sounds
move red decked legs quick and lean
step the step
slake the wine
blow de boo
canary yellow shades
valley of the yams
shake it up
ball de jack
do the thing
its your thing
cakewalking
into plumes of power

poem
tone place poem
about that blues bip bop
upside my head
happening
when i was least ready
and most open to

in the mist of bessie smith
i saw an old time movie
a man in a yam colored suit
black and happy
white buck shoes
white buck teeth
walking down that yellow dog road
a model t yellow cab blinking on and off
rolling sand vapor down the wooden road

and mamie
talkin   about that pot of cabbage
a boiling   overflowing
when the stick of bacon
came inside
almost overflowed the top
that salty dog
come on in

a marching band
over the delta land
thru time
thru space
thru thin dollar bills
thru death

reach thru space
thru a giant vaseline jar
come and get that memory

Big Red

tome tone tone
tone red fuzz of fire
jackal head
machine gun tongue
hot words   go upside
yo head.
big red now dead
screamed thru facile wires
his energy challenged electricity
sound waves break sound barriers
broke
light years
of fear

Biafra Stew Inc.

1

on storecounters of the seasonal rushes
tin can bellies of biafran babies
a crying commodity on the world market
next to the cash register
  a para institution
next to campbells soup
  tears slick on petroleum rivers
camp   hula hoops   the Charleston
pop art
all those things we can remember
  a cause
  of which causes are made

the contract was in pig latin
africans can only understand drums
five fingers fuck one pencil
over the closing of certain doors
the opening of others

recalled
from the freeway
one hundred thousand automobiles
dropped dead in their tracks/
when the land fails
mass movement down the peninsula
disembodied fossils fount to the skies
on the freeway

when
the deal goes down
the black cult of the pentagonal brotherhood
will remove the pope from his throne
he will hide out in jerusalem

plastered against the wailing wall
his hair will go to make brick for the temple
that will never be rebuilt
while fixing the patterns of life
on the dead sea.

2

the tubby truckdriver comes into the supermarket
his potbelly peeking out of his tee shirt
mock white grease of adding machines
he say
      i sends me boy outs to get some good ol dinty moore beef stew
      and when i gets ready to dig me chops in it   i find
      a whole lots of squiggling black babies
      crying and looking pitiful
      bellies big as
      basketballs

five black babies label a can
doing
the coon can
the coon can
         bellies big as basketballs

the crowd swarmed out of the subways
and across the brooklyn bridge
ten thousand black teenyboppers say
WE DONT WANT TO GO TO SCHOOL ON MOSES' BIRTHDAY
the cops stood lines of white helmets
they all ran down the street
at each other /   away from each other
and disappeared
in a funnel swirling wind and dust
thru endless time

below the tropic of cancer
along the peninsula

beyond the sea of galilee
five black babies
in a silver can
of stew

Sonny Rollins

sonny rollins seeking
peace in the city
jamming with
the subway train
a free rhythm section
coney island beach on the bridge
of hart crane /
"the most important thing to me
is my sanity"
refrain

The Jackal-headed Madonna

wanton de monster
a little menstrual blood
by sway of de moon
droplets on mama earth
donation for new babies and old men
droplets on the earth
scorch the soil

big face
lips puckered
jackal-headed madonna
chasing the white race
to their final enclave
in the catacombs of europa
a crag off mainline
ejaculate
ink of toil
cultures drop dead
a dick with no sap

on the front page
of the daily news
coming off page of the plane
onto the planet
with pussy galore
front page tabloid bopping
shades
resemblance thru pointillism
to an islamic soothsayer
we all knew oncet

the headlines spoke of a gynecological eclipse
in the sociological asphalt of a fortress
not there   but   outwhere

gin and dry ice

cracked with denmark beer
from technological duress
a certain loss of consciousness on the in bib
mornings of a clearness
coming thru the blood
lsd strontium 90 in the wards of the blood and soil

in young cuba
we walk the hill
or sit in the cafe
and watch the eastern sky daze
here or there   —outwhere

we lay
as we lay
each to our own bones
harken
the morning light
thru the scent of shades
food that is no use
for the juttings of the brain

in the ballroom of cannabis
sprawled on the floor
a ceremony
for the absence of ceremony
protestant now no longer   but
                         searching for a love
searching
searching
            in sociological debris
nightmares of fanon
in tv dining rooms
and the wretched shall inherit the earth /

sue the clinicians
logical sisters of western stars
means of debris and analysis
in the 33rd degree percentile

123

strung out on the network
of institutional vertigo programs for space
and the pummeling of the center of the earth
the darrows hobbits and elves
work in the lab
light up red dots all over the planet
when the door is open
the bells also chime

lets take an attitude
break it down the limbs of trees
the language of mankind
mumbo-jumbo
fuck the shit out of it

what we see from the third position
with the third eye
jump cyclopean strength
to the tune of the populace commonplace
the witches and warlocks
loom to groom the same
loom
outwhere

he handled his sonic type machine
with the hands of a basketball player
prestidigitatory big hands clap
DO IT NOW
the fingers snapped
a roomful of people
fell out de door

The Kenny Clark Blues or Jamboree

For Ishmael Reed

de police station wus crowded
folks an reporters wus all aroun
de police done caught poor kenny
with a hot xerox machine full o dope.

his mama said he had gone to work
his mama said he do good work
kenny mama said he didnt use no dope
but the big chief said there was no hope.

kenny clark sat in de corner
red wus his eyes blue wus his gums
his eyeballs goin up into his brain
kenny clark was the meanest coon in town

seems he had been doing the nod in de chinese restaurant
and when his face fell in his chop suey plate
de waiter thought he had died and he call de police
when de police come and see ol kenny they was afeared to touch him
cause kenny was the meanest coon in town
                    the meanest coon in town

de police called the big chief
and as wus expected
as soon as kenny was woke
he went for his big forty fo

but the big chief had the drop on him
and kenny wus no fool
he said lets go sit in my caddy
get nice and be cool

poor kenny poor kenny
what was he to do

soon as they left the restaurant
kenny realized that he had blew

there stood his caddy
big xerox in de back
bustin with packs of heroin

kenny clark said to the big chief
look like you got me at last
i aint had time to stash
and i'm too high to run

slick kenny went for his twenty-two
beat the big chief to the draw
but befo he could pull the trigger
he nodded out and started to snore

they call him kenny the coon
they call him kenny the coon
cause with his thick glasses on
and his eyes like half moon
kenny look jus like a sneaky raccoon

o kenny's mama was dere
holdin a burnin candle in his name
she sprinkled goofer dust all over the court
snapped her fingers stomped her feet
called on whats-his-name to do it now
wrote the judge name backwards on a dollar bill
and flushed it down the toilet

kenny clark was lined up handcuffed fingerprinted and mugged
but he was still
the meanest coon in town
the meanest coon in town

slick kenny pulled out a dope needle loaded to the brim
his eyes opened wide and his tongue flapped out
and he jugged the needle in

before he died from the overdose
kenny clark was heard to say
that was the best dope i ever done had

cause he was the meanest coon in town
the meanest coon in town
ol   kenny clark was the meanest coon in town

his mama cried she cried lawd she cried
she said
since daddy died
lawd since daddy died
nobody know the trouble i had
since daddy been dead

Harlem Anthropology

for the late Zora Neale Hurston

harlem you got some big legs!
some would call you a mystery
of dark peoples
living lost in time   / absent
some say
you would go with anyone
for a good time
                    (thats what othello said)
some say you are a violent   motherfucker
like to cut with razors
like to splash with lye
some
anthropologist say
that the razor scars so often found on harlem citizens
are reminiscent of their tribal heritage
where decorative marks on the body
were signs of beauty